The
CORPS
of
CADETS

The
CORPS
of
CADETS

A Year at West Point

Robert Stewart

With a Foreword by
Gen. Edward C. Meyer, USA (Ret.)

NAVAL INSTITUTE PRESS   ANNAPOLIS, MARYLAND

Library of Congress Cataloging-in-Publication Data

Stewart, Robert, 1949—
    The corps of cadets : a year at West Point / Robert Stewart ; with foreword by Edward C. Meyer.
      p.   cm.
    ISBN 1-55750-789-9 (alk. paper)
    1. United States Military Academy.   2. United States Military Academy—Pictorial works.
      I. Title.
U410.PIS74   1996
355'.0071'173—dc20   95-47752

Printed in Canada on acid-free paper ∞

03 02 01 00 99 98 97 96 9 8 7 6 5 4 3 2

First printing

This book is dedicated to 2d Lt. Paul W. Davison, U.S. Army,
U.S. Military Academy Class of 1995, with my gratitude for his valuable assistance.
Beginning with the USMA Class of 1885, Davison family members have
graduated from West Point and have served their country in the profession
of arms for five generations. I hope that Paul enjoys an exceptional career as an
Army officer and that he continues the proud traditions of The Long Gray Line
and his family's service to the nation.

FOREWORD

The U.S. Military Academy is a crucible of leadership. It is a place whose total focus is on the mental, physical, and moral aspects of shaping the lives of young men and women. This photographic documentary of West Point by Robert Stewart provides you with a pictorial and narrative insight into this unique institution—its cadets and their development, West Point's infrastructure, academic classes, traditions and ceremonies, athletics, military training, and its rockbound highland beauty. The kaleidoscope of photographs presented in this book will bring back memories for graduates, as well as help others have a better understanding of "Why a Military Academy?"

There is a line in the song "Dog Face Soldier" by Irving Berlin in which a young GI wails, "They're tearing me down to build me over again." At West Point, little tearing down is needed because the cadets who are selected to attend already demonstrate excellent mental and physical capabilities. They are *in the Army* while at West Point. They are also *in college.* This places a great demand on them and their time as they seek a degree and a commission. In addition to their mental and physical development, cadets also must develop ethically. Simply stated, the purpose of the Military Academy is to develop individuals of character who are dedicated to a lifetime of service to nation.

Cadet development continues to evolve to meet the changing needs of the Army. At West Point, standards for leadership in the rest of the Army are being developed and passed on to ROTC and OCS as the basis for their leadership development programs. Although our changing world also means changes at West Point, the core instruction and the focus on honor and concern for others continue to ensure that graduates are ready to lead as officers in the Army. Chapels dominate the skyline at West Point; the opportunity for cadets of all denominations to worship in accordance with their beliefs is present. Playing fields dominate the periphery of the academic buildings and dormitories; cadets must also actively participate in athletics. A sound mind in a sound body is practiced, not just preached.

For nearly two hundred years the Military Academy has been turning out military leaders. Some of its graduates have become presidents, ambassadors, leaders of industry, and outstanding leaders in all paths of life. The wide breadth of photographic scenes presented in *The Corps of Cadets: A Year at West Point* symbolize the Academy's goal of emphasizing the principles of Duty, Honor, and Country. It is this emphasis which enables West Point to continue developing young men and women of character who will lead and serve their nation.

Gen. Edward C. Meyer, USA (Ret.)
Chief of Staff, U.S. Army 1979–1983
USMA Class of 1951

INTRODUCTION

The U.S. Military Academy at West Point is located in a quiet and somewhat remote part of New York state, high above the Hudson River. During America's battle for independence, Gen. George Washington recognized that this area was a strategically important place at which the Revolutionary Army must turn back the advancing British forces.

More than two centuries later, when I spent fifteen months at the Academy to photograph and write about the institution and the Corps of Cadets, I realized that the somber gray walls of West Point's buildings and its geographical remoteness disguise the importance that the Academy still has for our society. West Point's graduates will be protectors of our nation's freedoms. This sometimes puts them in the dangerous role of being peacekeepers on foreign terrain in the post–Cold War world. They stand a sizeable watch in Europe and Asia to ensure that America's foreign interests are secure. Their countrymen trust them to be able, confident leaders in the profession of arms should war come or when peace prevails.

I always enjoyed talking to the cadets, a convincing and articulate lot of young people. They look directly at you when they speak, and their message is an assured one. They believe in themselves and in their calling. Cadets are as modest as they are determined. They laugh easily at themselves because preserving a sense of humor is necessary if one expects to tolerate the rigors of a military environment. Cadets are particularly friendly with and appreciative of anyone who wants to learn more about them, their Academy, and the imposing responsibilities that they and their classmates have sworn to discharge after they graduate.

Academy officials speak firmly about leadership when they discuss their institution's central aims. And if you ask a cadet to name the premier traits each and every cadet must exemplify as they prepare to be Army officers, he or she will usually mention leadership first. The subject is so essential that while its concepts are taught in a military context, the Academy emphasizes how it should be cultivated, modeled, and practiced in all other aspects of a person's life. West Point's goals are rooted in a steadfast belief that others will follow with conviction a leader who has character and integrity as sturdy as the mission.

First as Plebes, then throughout their four years at the Academy, all cadets learn that every encounter happens specifically for developmental purposes. The environment at West Point is designed to turn a raw new cadet into a disciplined and selfless person, classmate, and, eventually, capable U.S. Army officer.

Some members of Congress are currently asking openly whether the United States needs service academies anymore. They contend that the federal government should stop financing educations for military officers from West Point and the other service academies because the Cold War has ended. With their words and their actions, however, cadets showed me how their presence can disarm anyone who suggests that America should eliminate its service academies. Having talked candidly among the cadets while they were on the military training field, in classrooms, at athletic competitions, and during informal situations, I found them to be proud that they were selected and grateful for the outstanding education they receive. Moreover, cadets clearly understand the expectations their neighbors and their nation have of them. They accept their responsibilities seriously and are dedicated to them as students of their historic institution and as tomorrow's Army officers.

The days and evenings I spent among the Corps of Cadets were truly memorable. They are an impressive assembly of young men and women. The country is fortunate to have them as its sons and daughters.

Robert Stewart

The
CORPS
of
CADETS

I

FOURTH-CLASS YEAR

"Life at West Point is a journey, not a destination.
Your experiences and skills there transcend undergraduate academics.
You learn about people, time management, group dynamics, having a sense of
urgency, honor, and responsibility. You become an adult."

Maj. Phillip D. Macklin, USA, USMA '79

1926

For each new cadet class at the U.S. Military Academy, life begins near the end of June on R-Day, or Reception Day, and continues the tradition of The Long Gray Line at West Point. Recent cadet classes have consisted of approximately eleven- to twelve-hundred candidates—including two hundred minority members—who have been selected from a pool of more than thirteen thousand applicants. Women, who were admitted to the Academy in 1976 by congressional order and graduated starting with the Class of 1980, average 14 percent of each new class.

Candidates are drawn from two main classifications: 75 percent from congressional appointments and 25 percent from Department of the Army–designated categories. The latter includes presidential-level appointments; enlisted members of the regular Army, Army Reserve, and Army National Guard; the children of deceased or disabled veterans and Medal of Honor recipients; and persons enrolled in an Army Reserve Officers Training Corps program. Candidates represent every state in the Union, as well as a few foreign countries, such as the Republic of Korea, Turkey, Honduras, Cameroon, and Trinidad.

Typically, candidates ranked in the top fifth of their high school classes and received high scores on academic achievement tests. Many were also class valedictorians, National Merit Scholarship finalists, and members of the National Honor Society. Most new cadets excelled in interscholastic sports, served on their school publications staffs, held offices in student government, or achieved in all three of these extracurricular areas. Candidates must also meet rigorous physical and medical qualifications.

Each candidate arrives at West Point with just a few possessions: medical records, one small piece of luggage, basic grooming supplies, a wristwatch, a pair of athletic shoes, and one pair of "broken-in," laced, plain-toe, smooth-surface black leather shoes. Simplicity is the rule of the day. The Military Academy issues cadets what they will need for their lives there, from R-Day through every day of their four years at West Point.

New cadet "in-processing" commences at 6:30 A.M. The first candidates processed are graduates of the U.S. Military Academy Preparatory School, USMAPS, located at Fort Monmouth, New Jersey. The ten-month program there prepares selected applicants to enter West Point. Although these cadets must compete with all other candidates for admission, they have the advantage of a year's experience in the Army's culture. In fact, some of them have even had prior enlisted service as soldiers in the U.S. Army. As many as 15 percent of some incoming classes have been USMAPS graduates; 4 percent of them have had prior enlisted service.

Reception Day officially starts as new cadets and their family members are briefed in Holleder Center about the day's events and Cadet Basic Training, called CBT. The next time new cadets and relatives will meet is on Visiting Day, during the summer, and at the Acceptance Parade in August, when the new cadet class is officially accepted by the upperclass members of the Corps of Cadets as the new academic year begins.

Good-byes said, the new cadets head off for Arvin Gym, where USMA admissions staff check them in. Then they proceed through scheduled checkpoints. They are issued their uniforms and equipment and undergo medical screenings. Next, they learn the Oath of Allegiance—which they will officially swear to later that day on the Plain, the Academy's parade field—followed by a fitness test of pull-ups. Before they leave the gym, new cadets receive their unit assignment. Later, in the basement barbershop at Washington Hall, the men have their heads shaved and women have their hair trimmed to collar length.

Between mid-morning and mid-afternoon, Central Area is occupied with clusters of new cadets and upperclass cadets who are the members of the Cadet Cadre for CBT. Central Area is surrounded by the Pershing, Eisenhower, and Bradley Barracks and the rear of Washington Hall. Incoming cadets stand at attention on what is typically a hot and humid day, outfitted in Academy-issued athletic shirts and shorts, knee-length black socks, and their own plain-toe black dress shoes. Perspiration covers their foreheads and streams down their cheeks as the temperatures combine with the day's suspense. Each new cadet must first "Report to the cadet in the red sash," the garment that identifies upperclass cadets standing in Central Area. These upperclass cadets check the tags attached to the new cadets' athletic shorts to verify that he or she has been through all the required checkpoints since leaving Arvin Gym.

The following notes about R-Day events have been excerpted from the diary of a new cadet. Many other West Point graduates will identify with this record of "the way it was."

First Question of the Day: Do I wear the black shoes or regular shoes? I decided to go to Ames and pick up a cheap pair of jeans to go with the black shoes and be on the safe side. My decision caused me to be one of the last New Cadets to report.

Report to Holleder Center. The cadre made us say good-bye in 5 minutes. Every mom was crying. On the bus down to Arvin no one spoke. Everyone looked nervous.

Arvin Gym. On our own. Changed into R-Day uniform (Gym A with black socks and shoes). Did lots of paperwork, took pills and shots, fitted for T-shirts and shorts, did pull ups, got briefed on Cadet Honor Code.

Haircuts and Issue points in Washington Hall basement. We got these huge barracks bags that were WAY too heavy. All this happened so we would be sweaty and confused before we got to our Beast Company.

Reception. The first time we were really yelled at. We learned salutes, the position of attention, four responses.

Cadet in the Red Sash. Reported to him, usually got the words wrong while reporting. Followed many tape trails up to the new Company. Everyone got lost. When you finally made it up to the Company and were told to go back to the CDT in the Red Sash, he checked your tags a million times to make sure you reported to all the right issue points, learned to drill, went to your room, etc.

Report to the First Sergeant (1SG). Signed into CDT Company. Memorized a paragraph before going in to report. This was the most frightening part of the day because all one could hear was yelling, and stressed-out New Cadets, coming out of the room. Attention to detail was stressed.

Finally made it to my room. Dropped the huge bag I was issued. Drank water, as ordered, and went to the bathroom. I met my roommate briefly.

Lunch. I went to the last lunch session. We had hamburgers, that's all I remember. The nine of us at the table were told to look around because that was the last time we would be able to look around until March.

Drill 1 and Drill 2. I was supposed to go to two drill sessions to learn all facing movements and how to march, but because I reported so late, I had no time to drill. My roommate taught me how to do the facing movements in our room 20 minutes before the parade. I was lucky, though, because it rained during drill for everyone else.

We got ready for the parade in our White Over Gray uniform. Everyone had stuff on wrong so it took my squad about an hour just to get ready. I think we drank about a gallon of water before the parade. All we could hear was "Drink water, New Cadets," or "New Cadets, get on my wall, NOW."

Parade. By now it was 5 P.M. and we lined up for the parade. All the cadre were upset about something, anything we did. Nothing went the way it was supposed to. Somehow we ended up on the parade field and took the oath. We had one glove on and we were carrying the other. At the end of the parade we marched into the Mess Hall and began dinner.

Dinner. Everyone had to look at their plate, or the squad leader (a junior upperclass cadet who fulfills a NCO position during CBT). No one talked. We took small bites. We all made tons of mistakes and learned the proper way to present the food at the table and do our table duties. The squad leader stressed teamwork and motivation. It was not a fun meal.

The day wasn't over. We had to fix our rooms, make our beds, drink more water, learn the chain of command, learn Beast knowledge, let alone get to know each other. There was too much to do in too little time. Lights out and Taps were at 2200, 10 P.M. for those of us who wanted to remember what it was like to be civilian. Welcome to West Point.

At this point, the Academy's newest class members are taught how to salute, how to stand at attention the West Point way, and how to perform the left, right, and about-face turns that they will execute during CBT and throughout Plebe year. New cadets are permitted only four responses, in this sequence: "Yes, sir/ma'am. No, sir/ma'am. No excuse, sir/ma'am. Sir/Ma'am, I do not understand." The reason for restricting new cadet responses is stated in the CBT *Trainer's Guide.* "Cadets must cultivate the habit of not offering excuses which divert responsibility for one's action. There is no place in the military for an excuse for failure. Extenuating circumstances may be explained . . . but are never considered excuses."

Each new cadet must then report again to a Cadet Cadre member in a red sash, who confirms that he or she learned everything correctly. If they did not, they are sent back to complete any of the stations that they did not finish as expected, or to learn again. The ones who pass this traditional muster of the second report proceed to the tables under the sally ports—the archways that connect the Central Area and the Plain—to learn their company designation, after which they move on to their barracks and report to the first sergeant on their proper floor. At this step of R-Day, the new cadet signs in to his or her company and learns the names of the CBT platoon and squad leaders who are responsible for new cadet orientation and development.

"If you can keep your sense of humor,
keep from taking yourself too seriously,
and believe that 'this too shall pass,'
you can make it through Cadet Basic Training."

Richard Sonstelie, USMA '66

At the top of the list in that orientation is learning some important West Point vernacular. Freshmen are Plebes, or fourth-class cadets; sophomores are Yearlings, or third-class cadets; juniors are Cows, or second-class cadets; and seniors are Firsties, or first-class cadets. Plebe comes from the Latin *pleb*, meaning lowest class. Yearling originated from an unknown source sometime between the 1850s and the 1870s. Cow came from the post–Civil War period, and Firstie was adopted during Col. Sylvanus Thayer's tenure as Academy superintendent (1817–33).

At approximately 5:30 P.M. on Reception Day the newest class members march onto the Plain to swear the Oath of Allegiance. With their right hands raised, following the orders of the Commandant of Cadets, they repeat:

> I, (name), do solemnly swear that I will support the Constitution of the United States, and bear true allegiance to the National Government; that I will maintain and defend the sovereignty of the United States, paramount to any and all allegiance, sovereignty, or fealty I may owe to any State or country whatsoever; and that I will at all times obey the legal orders of my superior officers, and the Uniform Code of Military Justice.

That pledge to obey superior officers begins with CBT, when the new cadet makes the transition from civilian to soldier-cadet and in so doing builds self-confidence and self-esteem. Some of the program's principal aims are military and basic soldiering skills, physical fitness, self-discipline, time management, teamwork, leadership, and the ability to function under pressure. West Pointers traditionally call these first six weeks of rigorous training "Beast Barracks." This is an important time for new cadets to learn about honor, the scope of Academy life, conduct, history, traditions, and regulations. When CBT is over, and the academic year starts, these new cadets will be promoted to the rank of cadet private, will be officially accepted into the Corps of Cadets, and will be called Plebes.

Company commanders for CBT are first-class members of the Cadet Cadre who are directly responsible for new cadet training. Each company has approximately 130 to 150 new cadets. The ratio between Cadet Cadre officer and new cadet gets smaller at the platoon level, and the most interaction between leaders and subordinates occurs at the squad level, with approximately eight to ten new cadets assigned to a squad.

Cadet Cadre instructors are expected to motivate and communicate to each new cadet the goals of West Point and service to the Army and to the nation. The Cadet Cadre are Cows and Firsties who are considered models of leadership and follow the Cadet Leader Development System Guide. Members of the Cadet Cadre at CBT must know the developmental purpose and value for any order they issue to a new cadet. A member's words and actions should be consistent with the professional and personal character traits they teach to the new cadets in their charge.

"Every American should appreciate that West Point graduates, even those who do not choose a lifetime career in the military, contribute far more back to the strength of our military system—as well as their communities, businesses, and our political system— than the cost of the education they received."

Danna Maller, USMA '80

* * *

The basic training is divided into two three-week sessions—Details I and II—which are both conducted at the Academy. While Details I and II are almost identical, Detail II includes more field training. The Cadet Cadre officers who lead Detail I are replaced by upperclass cadets who have returned to West Point after being at home on leave or attending either military or academic Individual Advanced Development. This includes programs such as Airborne and Air Assault School, academic trips, and summer elective courses.

Reveille for Details I and II is normally at 5:45 A.M., but new cadets must rise even earlier to perform duties like delivering newspapers and studying. They rise at 5:20 A.M. and line up thirty minutes later in their companies in front of Washington Hall. The Detail's regimental commander calls all companies to report just before the American flag is raised. When they are dismissed, the new cadet companies move out immediately to the Plain with their platoon and squad leaders, three days a week, for PT, or physical training, that lasts more than an hour and ends with a three-mile run across the Academy grounds.

On the two other mornings (and the afternoons of those same days), new cadets practice marching and close-order drills with their rifles. In the late afternoon every day they again participate in athletic competitions on the Plain. When the new cadets are not participating in morning PT, late-day athletics, or close-order drill, they spend considerable time—dressed in camouflage fatigues, or BDUs (Battle Dress Uniform)—learning about West Point's customs, organization, rules, and mission. They receive honor instruction, study the cadet discipline system, and take social training on new cadet etiquette and fourth-class privileges.

"Life at West Point begins before dawn and lasts forever."

Jack Reed, U.S. Congress 2nd District, Rhode Island, USMA '71

New cadet development continues with explicit instruction about the way they must conduct themselves at all times during CBT when they are on the Post (the entire area behind West Point's gates). When an officer or upperclass cadet enters a new cadet's room, the new cadet will come to attention, call all other cadets in the room to attention, and report, "Sir/Ma'am, New Cadet _____, _____ squad, _____ platoon, reports." Most CBT rules likewise apply to fourth-class cadets when the academic year begins.

There are many rules. New cadets must walk at a brisk pace whenever they are near the barracks, out of doors, or not in formation. They cannot speak to classmates while they are in barracks halls or stairways or while performing duties unless they first obtain permission from an upperclass cadet in the area.

Throughout CBT, new cadets keep one item with them at all times, or at least within easy reach. It is *Bugle Notes,* the chief encyclopedic source of information about various USMA and U.S. Army subjects: the Office of the Commandant of Cadets and his chain of command; cadet rank insignia; academic departments; extracurricular activities; athletics; general information about senior Department of Defense officials, insignia of rank, awards and decorations, Army badges and tabs; West Point heritage, legends, and traditions; a glossary of cadet slang. Most important are the definitions of West Point's three guiding missions—Duty, Honor, Country.

*"I remember distinctly the amount of time I spent in 'laughing locker'
with Fred Barofsky, still a dear friend and a true leader.
Freddy and I could never stand ranks at any formation in our
Beast Squad without smirking. Nothing in my life was more funny
than being forced to spend time, nose to nose, with Fred.
I still can't do it without smirking."*

Thomas B. Dyer, USMA '67

During CBT—and later, when they are Plebes—new cadets are required daily to
master certain information no later than breakfast formation. This includes: the menu for
breakfast, lunch, and dinner; the name, branch, and unit of assignment of the officer-in-
charge; current events (that is, all relevant front-page and sports-page news); and, of
course, "The Days." In this long-standing tradition, every fourth-class cadet must recite:

> Sir/Ma'am, the days. Today is (day of the week and date). There are
> (number) and a butt days until Ring Weekend for the Class of _____;
> there are (number) and a butt days until Army defeats (home football
> opponent for that week) at Michie Stadium in football; there are (num-
> ber) and a butt days until Army beats the hell out of Navy in football;
> there are (number) and a butt days until Christmas leave for the United
> States Corps of Cadets; there are (number) and a butt days until 500th
> night; there are (number) and a butt days until 100th night; there are
> (number) and a butt days until Yearling winter weekend; there are (num-
> ber) and a butt days until spring leave for the upper three classes; there
> are (number) and a butt days until graduation and graduation leave for
> the Class of _____, Sir/Ma'am.

As the site of many activities such as banquets and rallies throughout the year, the Cadet Mess is a central location at West Point. Moreover, it is an environment where senior-subordinate relationships are practiced, naturally.

After entering the mess, new cadets stand at "attention" behind their chairs until they are ordered to "take seats." They remain at attention while seated: sitting upright, their backs straight—not touching the back of their chair—their feet flat on the floor. They do not talk except in the presence of an upperclass cadet, and after they have received permission to do so.

During CBT, new cadets have explicit duties and rules they must follow at mess. Their squad leader is usually the table commandant for his or her new cadets. The first new cadet duty post at mess is to be the gunner. When all cadets have been served, the gunner will announce, "Sir/Ma'am, there are _____ servings of _____ remaining on the table." The gunner also announces when additional supplies are on the table, cuts the dessert according to the required number of pieces, and calls out other commands. The cold beverage corporal sits at the end of the table opposite the table commandant, announces the preferred beverage for the meal, serves it, and keeps the table supplied with it. He or she likewise announces, "Sir/Ma'am, the new cadets at this table have performed their duties and are now prepared to eat." (A hot beverage corporal keeps the table supplied with soup as well as tea, coffee, or hot chocolate.)

Detail II ends with the new cadets conducting a week-long bivouac at Lake Frederick, near West Point. There they set up in a seven-hundred-tent city and participate in various field competitions. The week concludes with Organization Day, when social, athletic, and military events showcase the spirit of the new cadet class. Organization Day occurs the day before the twelve-mile foot march back to West Point, as CBT ends and the fall academic period approaches.

*"I was a second lieutenant, an infantry platoon leader in August of 1990. . . .
As my unit prepared for deployment to Saudi Arabia, three of my young soldiers and
their wives approached me and asked, 'Sir, what do you think will happen if we go to war?'
Though not yet fully comfortable in my own role—which was only weeks old—I answered,
'We'll all be just fine. You guys are better than you think you are,
and we'll take care of each other.' During that moment, I realized that
I had adopted the leadership persona which I had begun forming
several years earlier as a Plebe at West Point."*

Mark M. Jennings, USMA '89

* * *

Reorganization Week happens in mid-August, as all the upperclass cadets return to West Point after summer military training. They arrive and prepare for two tasks: first, the academic period, and second, slightly more than one thousand unknown, untested new cadets.

On Acceptance Day the new cadets are officially "accepted" into the U.S. Corps of Cadets. Now they are Plebes, not new cadets. But the days ahead will still be tough for them. They must go through many more issue points than they did on R-Day, receiving textbooks and class schedules and other materials. They must also learn the names and faces of some ninety upperclass cadets in their respective companies. They are not granted leave to go home before the academic period starts. Most of all, the tensions of Plebe life don't ease up just because Beast Barracks is over. In fact, with the Youngsters, Cows, and Firsties back, things get tougher.

The regulations that govern Plebe conduct during the academic period are clear. The military atmosphere of self-discipline, personal conduct, and responsibility established during CBT continues when classes begin. Plebes address all upperclass cadets as "Sir" or "Ma'am." When they are in cadet areas excluding academic buildings, they must walk in an erect military manner. Company officers make sure their Plebes are in ranks for all corps, regimental, and company formations five minutes prior to assembly, but not earlier. Occasions are exceedingly rare when they can stand "at ease."

Plebes also know they cannot speak to classmates when they are in the barracks hallways or while they walk in any cadet area unless they are performing official duties. They are not permitted to wear civilian clothing anywhere on the Post, nor can they date upperclass cadets. During their first term, Plebes are not allowed to have record players, stereos, tape decks, or radios in their rooms.

Clothing restrictions for fourth-class cadets are explicit. They must wear a complete uniform—determined by the weather and the season—at all times. This means even the hours between 7:30 P.M. and taps at 11:30, although for that period the uniform can be the Gym Alpha, or sweat suit with athletic shoes.

In the barracks, new cadets are mail carriers, minute callers, runners, laundry deliverers, and orderlies, in addition to performing company duties that are prescribed by their own chains of command. A minute caller, for example, announces the time remaining before assembly for all formations. Throughout the Academy's barracks, they stand at attention at designated posts and shout out such traditional announcements as: "Attention all cadets, there are _____ minutes until haircut inspection and lunch formation. The uniform is As For Class, under short overcoat. _____ minutes remaining."

The Cadet Leadership Development System at West Point has actually instituted some noteworthy changes concerning a cadet's bearing and posture. Today's Plebes are not required to square corners, that is, make a 90-degree turn anywhere they walk inside or outside the Post. They do not have to get up against a wall, hug a wall, or "ping," which means moving from one place to another at a jog. In fact, regulations forbid these and other forms of exaggerated posture, movement, or bearing by any cadet. Incoming cadets (and the Plebes they will become) are not expected to walk faster, straighter, or more militarily than upperclass cadets. Many at West Point believe that these changes symbolize progressive attitudes and a more constructive approach to cadet development.

Minute callers repeat their announcements five, four, three, and two minutes before formation. When calling the two-minute bell, they might use this address: "Attention all cadets, there are two minutes until assembly for morning quarters formation. The uniform is White Over Gray. This is the last minute to be called for this formation. Do not forget your lights. Two minutes remaining."

"Plebes need uncommon perseverance," said one Firstie, "because they must accomplish many tasks, not just for one day, but for the entire year." West Point's highly regimented atmosphere, plus the constraints of fourth-class life, offer advantages and disadvantages. "It's hard when you're home during leave. You're with your high school friends who go to civilian colleges, and they seem ahead of you in social skills and experiences," remarked one Firstie about the first months at West Point. But, he emphasized, cadets have certain other experiences that accelerate their maturity. "We cultivate invaluable leadership skills. We have audiences with some of the country's leading public figures. Cadets attend receptions with the president or the Chief of Staff

of the Army or the Secretary of Defense. So in the end, it will be easier to learn social skills than it will be to learn the importance and value of leadership."

Plebes have to master three parts of Academy life if they want to make it at West Point. The first one is time management of academics and responsibilities. Plebes who manage their time are less likely to end up in trouble. The second part is attitude. A Plebe has to demonstrate a high spirit and not take anything personally when a upper-class cadet tries to make him or her uneasy or slip up. The third part is appearance. You'd better look squared away at all times. A Plebe with an appearance problem could attract a "Heat Magnet" (a Cow or a Firstie out looking for fourth-class cadets whose appearance will not pass inspection). Cows are famous for being tough on Plebes, while Yearlings—each of whom has a Plebe or two to mentor—are usually supportive. That's why they often get called "Sugar Daddies."

Times were even stricter fifty years ago at the Academy. "In 1940 when I was a Plebe, we had to brace with our backs up against a wall when upperclassmen passed by. We had to double-time every place we went. We called the 'minutes' until formation, squared every perpendicular corner when we were out of barracks, and we had to keep a two-finger width at all times between the brim of our caps and our noses. It was tough to see under the brim of our full dress uniform hats." So said Col. George S. Pappas, USMA Class of 1944, eminent West Point historian and author of *To the Point: The United States Military Academy, 1802–1902.*

Pappas further describes that he and his classmates always had to look straight ahead, whether they were marching to class—they always marched to class—or sitting on the last two inches of their seats in the mess hall. They were not permitted to walk around the Post on their own. They could not go to Flirtation Walk and could not date. They had to double-time everywhere but that stopped when Beast Barracks ended. "But we did not dislike the Plebe system," he remarks. "We all realized we were on the bottom, and we did not resent the way we were treated. There were a couple of mean-spirited upperclassmen who seemed to have it out for Plebes. But for the most part, the upperclassmen always tried to teach us something purposeful."

Seven months after Reorganization Week, the Plebes are finally ready for "Recognition" by the upper classes during a ceremony connected to Founders' Day. The companies form in their regimental areas, and the Plebe class of each company lines up, single file, in front. The upperclass cadets file past, introduce themselves by their first names, and shake hands with the Plebes. Now, they can "fall out" like everyone else does when they are dismissed. The Plebes pin the "U.S." insignia on their bare shirt collars and mark their promotion from cadet private to cadet private first class.

II

LIFE AT THE
U. S. MILITARY
ACADEMY

"USMA is more than just a university, although it does provide an unbeatable education. . . .
The experience teaches attention to detail, discipline, loyalty, and unwavering integrity.
It is not optional to learn these qualities. You learn them and live them
or you leave West Point."

Capt. Kristin M. Baker, USA, USMA '90

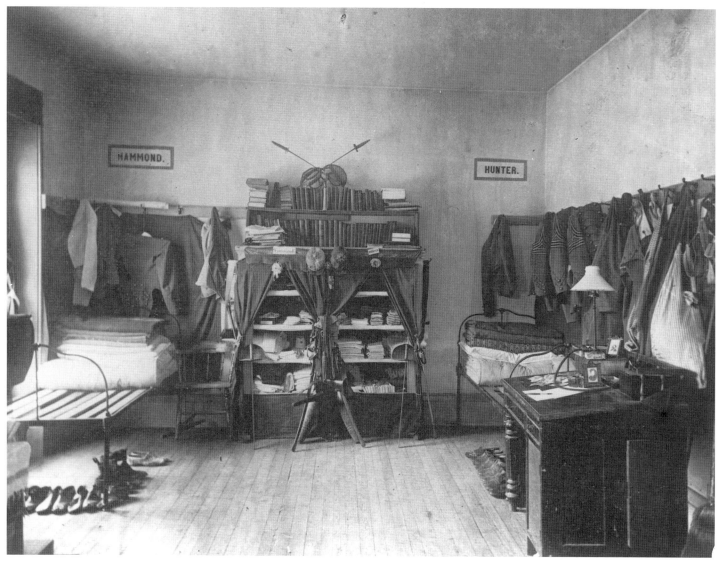

1877

V irtually every day except Sunday, life for West Point cadets is tightly organized and governed by firm schedules. Cadets feel that they never have enough time. Although civilian college students might complain that they face similar pressures, the Academy's regimentation and daily routines are still more demanding.

At 6:00 A.M., Monday through Friday, slightly more than four thousand cadets must rise, wash, dress in the uniform appropriate for the day and activity, and assemble outside for the first of the day's two formations, which precede breakfast and lunch. They live two and sometimes three to a room, in eight different barracks. Rooms are spartan and must be kept clean enough to pass inspection at any time. Cadets even resort to using a clipboard to tuck in the sheets and blanket, thus making them taut without lifting up the mattress. Formations include regular uniform inspections and weekly haircut inspections. Whether in rain or snow, sunshine or darkness, freezing or

1929

(U.S. MILITARY ACADEMY ARCHIVES)

sweltering temperatures, formations take place, the battalion commanders reporting in to their regimental commanders. After each formation the entire brigade marches into Cadet Mess in Washington Hall for their meals. They eat simultaneously at tables of ten, each cadet having an assigned seat.

Between 1815 and 1817, when Capt. Alden Partridge was superintendent, he ordered stiff regulations about mess. Cadets marched to and from the mess, honoring Partridge's edict that "the utmost order and silence must be observed in going and returning." He expected each table to be kept in perfect order. Talking was prohibited unless someone definitely had to ask for something. At every table, one cadet was assigned to "carve the victuals and help others to such as they may wish." When the meal was over, everyone was to "rise from table by word of Command, the carvers first, and return by files in the most perfect order."

Cadets still march to mess, but the Cadet Leader Development System guidelines describe that "Dining in the Cadet Mess should also contribute to development by providing opportunities for learning through interaction with peers and cadet leaders, inculcating social bonds and graces, and reinforcing table etiquette." After all the cadets have entered the mess hall, the brigade adjutant calls everyone to "Attention to Orders," makes a short announcement or two, and orders all cadets to "Take seats." Cadets sit and eat at the "rest" position, which is the prescribed standard for cadets of all four classes during meals. Upperclass cadets may talk to anyone; fourth-class cadets can talk to their classmates after they complete their table duties. A Plebe is not required to sit and eat more formally than any other cadet does.

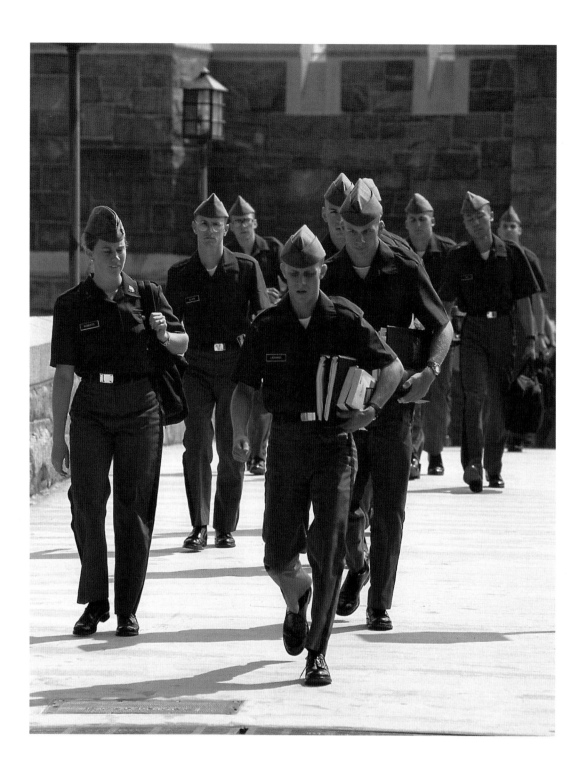

The first morning classes begin promptly at 7:15. These include academic lessons, military instruction, and physical education. Cadets attend four morning classes before they assemble again for noon formation followed by lunch. The afternoons are full of more classes, athletic practice (intercollegiate-varsity, club sports, or intramurals), cadet extracurricular activities, barracks duties, or work assignments with different Academy administrative departments. At 6:00 P.M. the sounding of retreat can be heard: a bugler plays as the American flag is lowered at sunset.

From the time that dinner ends until taps is played at 11:30 P.M., cadets study in their barracks or at the Academy library, coach other cadets in academic lessons, work with Plebes, and/or represent their class or company at various activities. The George S. Patton, Jr., Monument is located in front of the Academy library. The four silver

stars that General Patton wore, and one gold cavalry insignia that his wife wore throughout their marriage, were melted into the statue's bronze hands. Also located between the base and the pedestal of Patton's statue are four embroidered stars and a 3d Army shoulder patch from his uniform.

Cadets are awarded a Bachelor of Science degree when they graduate. The academic program's thirty-one-course core curriculum is founded on mathematics, the humanities, and the social, behavioral, and engineering sciences. Core courses include chemistry, computer science, economics, engineering science, English, foreign languages, history, mathematics, military history and leadership, literature, physics, political science, psychology, and international relations, among others. The Academy calls its core curriculum the "professional major" because it prepares each West Point graduate for a career as a commissioned U.S. Army officer. Academic officials and department chairpersons expect the core courses to address current professional, national, and international events as they reinforce the institution's guiding principles: Duty, Honor, Country.

The academic program is under the direct command of the Dean of the Academic Board, who is an Army brigadier general. The Academy's academic departments are: behavioral sciences and leadership; chemistry; civil and mechanical engineering; electrical engineering and computer science; English; foreign languages; geography and environmental engineering; history; law; mathematical sciences; physics; social sciences; and systems engineering. The instructional departments are physical education and military instruction.

To graduate from West Point, cadets need to satisfy the following academic criteria: (a) complete the baseline requirement of a field of study of forty academic courses, with an opportunity to voluntarily choose an optional major for which they complete an additional one to four courses; (b) complete or validate each course in the core curriculum; (c) pass eight semesters of physical education; (d) complete four military science sessions; and (e) earn a cumulative grade point average of 2.0 or higher. Besides completing baseline requirements, cadets may select elective programs during the last two years of academic study.

Fourth-class cadets complete academic studies that do not include elective courses. They must pass courses in English, literature, computer science, psychology, chemistry, math, and U.S. or world history. Third-class cadets also finish an academic plan without electives. They attend two semesters of a foreign language, physics, and math, in addition to semester-long courses in American politics, economics, philosophy, and terrain analysis. Second-class cadets take two semesters of military history, three semester-long courses in a designated engineering science, military leadership, international relations, and English, plus two electives. First-class cadets study constitutional law and attend two semester-long courses in a designated engineering design area. To graduate, all cadets must complete a five-course engineering sequence they select from seven engineering areas: civil, computer, electrical, environmental, mechanical, nuclear, and systems.

Cadets may either choose one of twenty-nine fields of study or one of nineteen optional majors, which are extended voluntary studies in a dedicated intellectual discipline. For most cadets, the path to graduation is the field of study program.

This emphasis on the sciences reflects the fact that West Point was originally established as an engineering school. In 1802, mathematics was the root of all academic

1903

1936

1952

*"Life at West Point is memorable and remarkable.
One day you are maxing 'boards,' the next day you are moaning about a
lousy summer assignment. One week you revel at the vast and vivid display
of fall colors in the Hudson Valley, the next week you retreat into the gray sky,
the grayer buildings, and your grayest uniform."*

Ellen W. Houlihan, USMA '82

instruction and remained so for more than 150 years. Cadets studied physics and mechanics and recited and discussed their lessons with instructors. Classes were small. Each student officer and cadet was expected to recite in class every day. The blackboard was a primary instrument for work and recitation. Instructors rarely lectured their cadet and officer students.

As the "Father of the Military Academy," Col. Sylvanus Thayer believed that the Academy should educate potential officers to perform in all branches of the Army—including the infantry and cavalry—not just the corps of engineers and artillery. Thayer established a system that permitted the educationally advanced cadets to progress faster by studying their subjects in more detail. He also introduced a system of numbering the classes that is still used today. The Plebe class was designated as the fourth class and the seniors were recognized as the first class. Thayer delegated enormous authority to professors and senior teachers regarding academic matters. Thayer Monument was erected in 1883 in memory of Colonel Thayer. It is located at a corner of the Plain, adjacent to the commandant's quarters.

The inscription on the statue reads:

COLONEL THAYER,
FATHER
OF THE
MILITARY ACADEMY

The current academic program operates with the latest information management systems. The cadets' personal computers in their rooms and the ones located in many classroom laboratories are supported by word processing, laser printing, worldwide electronic mail and bulletin boards, library bibliographic information, and statistical analysis and graphics software, among other aids. Approximately fifty-five hundred people at West Point use the Academic Computer Network. They send forty-five thousand electronic messages daily, while hundreds of electronic bulletin boards announce information about sports, academics, and special events.

Cadets who excel in academics are selected to receive prestigious scholarships for postgraduate studies. Since 1923, more than sixty-five Academy graduates have been awarded Rhodes scholarships to attend Oxford University while they are on active duty. West Point is the United States' fourth-ranked source of Rhodes scholars.

Each year two Military Academy graduates receive the George Olmstead Foundation annual award for two years of study at a foreign university where a language other than English is spoken. National Science Foundation Fellowships are awarded to outstanding cadets who pursue graduate study at a university of their choice. Hertz Foundation Fellowships are conferred on cadets to complete doctorates in applied physical science disciplines. The Marshall Scholarships program, established in 1953 by the British government, awards scholarships for two years of study to American university graduates with a baccalaureate. The Military Academy, which joined that program in 1983, has had numerous recipients since. The Harry S. Truman Foundation Scholarship is awarded to college juniors who have demonstrated a dedication to public service. West Point is one of the few universities in the United States that had two Truman scholars in successive years.

✳ ✳ ✳

The Department of Physical Education directs classroom training supported by intercollegiate athletics, club sports, and intramural activities.

Baseline requirements for cadets in the physical development program today include four components. The first component is physical education instruction, in which cadets complete a prescribed core of course work and skills practice in individual and team sports. Plebes engage in combative activities (boxing and wrestling for the men, self-defense for the women), swimming, and gymnastics. Upperclass cadets select from twenty courses to meet their mandatory and elective requirements. Some of those courses are volleyball, badminton, aerobic dance, bowling, scuba diving, and handball.

The second component is physical fitness testing. Cadets are required to pass the Cadet Physical Fitness Test twice a year during each of their four years at West Point.

Cadets must also finish the Indoor Obstacle Course Test during their third- and first-class years. When they become commissioned officers, they will be physically evaluated at scheduled times by the Army.

Third, cadets are required to participate either in intercollegiate athletics or corps squad, club squad, or company intramural team competition each academic semester. At the turn of the century, West Point didn't offer any club or intramural sports. Physical fitness activities included horseback riding and ice-skating and swimming (at the north side of the Post, near the Hudson River). The first intercollegiate sport was football, starting in 1890, and a game somewhat akin to baseball dates back to the 1820s.

Times have really changed. Today, at the intercollegiate level, men represent the Military Academy in seventeen competitive sports, and women in nine. Twenty-two competitive club squad sports are offered seasonally, including sailing, cycling, rowing, fencing, and equestrian and triathlon events. Cadets also can compete twice a week on intramural teams for area hockey, rugby, softball, racquetball, soccer, football, swimming, orienteering, boxing, and basketball for people 5'10" or shorter. Women's lacrosse and sport parachuting are club activities.

The Academy's intramural athletics program is an important dimension of the cadets' physical development plan. Each company is represented by one team in each sport. Regimental champion teams compete in playoffs at the end of each of the four intramural seasons for the honor of being the brigade champion. Every eligible cadet must participate in at least one intramural sport each semester. Each company is also

"In my Cow year, one of my roommates and I were academic coaches to two athletes: our other roommate, fullback George Pappas, and Bob Foley, a star basketball player from across the hall. One night after supper while we relaxed in our room, I loosened my trousers to accommodate the big meal I had eaten. There was a knock at the door, and the Commandant of Cadets, Brig. Gen. Richard G. Stilwell walked in. He had come to check on the academic progress of our charges. The moment I saw him, I arose instantly and called the room to attention. As I did, my trousers fell to my ankles. I had lost a great opportunity to impress the commandant."

Michael J. Bowers, Attorney General of Georgia, USMA '63

required to field a team in every sport each season. Cadets must participate in at least one team/contact sport during their four years at West Point. The intramural program is linked to the cadets' preparation as officers, especially on the battlefield, so that they are able and confident to lead soldiers as a member of a team.

The fourth required component is Master Fitness Training. When they graduate, all of the cadets will have the opportunity to be tested individually to earn the skill title of Master Fitness Trainer, a qualification that will permit them to develop and lead unit fitness programs in the Army.

While Yearlings and Cows do not have Plebe regs to worry about, they nevertheless concentrate on academics and leadership, which for Yearlings includes training their Plebes. An upperclass cadet commented, "The Academy environment is really a function of leadership for Yearlings and Cows. You work hard to pinpoint your own leadership style and how to effectively influence others and guide your Plebe."

Such leadership is intrinsic in the United States Corps of Cadets (USCC), a governing body that has substantial responsibilities and broad discretionary powers. The highest organizational level is the brigade, composed of approximately four thousand cadets. The brigade is divided into four regiments, with three battalions in each regiment. Each battalion has three companies (the level at which cadets officially identify themselves in the USCC chain of command), for a total of thirty-six companies in the brigade—with approximately 110 cadets per company. Each company comprises four platoons, twenty-five cadets per platoon, including the platoon sergeant and the platoon leader. Next are three squads per platoon, the squad size ranging from five to eight or ten cadets. Finally, there are two teams in each squad, with two or three cadets (usually a Yearling and one or two Plebes) per team.

Before the academic period starts, the Commandant of Cadets appoints one first-class cadet to lead the brigade for the whole academic year. This cadet, who holds the ranks of brigade commander and first captain, reports to the commandant, an Army brigadier general who is appointed by the President of the United States.

The first captain is a cadet who has earned outstanding achievements in many areas of responsibility and performance. He or she commands the brigade and directs a staff of cadet officers that includes a deputy commander, an executive officer, an adjutant, and officers with assistants who are in charge of the Corps' operations, activities, athletics, and supplies. A command sergeant major who is a second-class cadet also serves on the brigade staff.

Each company has a set of cadet staff officers. Their responsibilities include training, athletics, spirit, regulations and discipline, supply, personnel, and activities. Cadets plan and administrate most of their activities, such as pep rallies, designing their class ring and crest, cadet dances, and traditional ceremonies like the Ring Weekend events in August, when first-class cadets receive their class rings.

First-class cadets furnish overall leadership for the activities and operations of the USCC. Cadet captains and their staff command each of the four regiments, the twelve battalions, and the thirty-six companies; cadet lieutenants lead platoons. Cadet ranks begin with cadet private for fourth-class cadets and rise from corporal, sergeant, and first sergeant to sergeant major, lieutenant, and finally captain. A cadet's rank is identified by sleeve insignia on the uniform coat and parade-uniform jacket, shoulder epaulets, and collar bar insignia on all working uniforms of the day. The whole system emphasizes leadership by example. As is stated in the Cadet Leader Development System directive, "Subordinates cannot be held to higher standards than their leaders."

Every cadet's progress as a leader is evaluated. In the area of leader development, each cadet's academic, military, and physical performance is weighed. The score affects military branch selection and graduation sequence for some cadets. Leadership development is measured by a cadet's performance in the duty positions to which he or she has been assigned.

While its vision and mission are certainly unique, West Point responds like any university to students who have difficulties that affect their motivation and their accomplishments. Cadet leaders are trained to look for signs that indicate a subordinate is performing below standards for education, training, and military conduct. When they spot them, the cadet leaders must take remedial or corrective action. Several options are available. They can coach, instruct, or counsel the subordinate; they can refer the subordinate to remedial skills training; or they can report the subordinate to the next higher level in the USCC chain of command.

If appropriate, they can refer the situation to other external sources of assistance at the Academy after consulting with the tactical officer, or TAC, who is a commissioned Army officer. (There are also noncommissioned TACs.) The company TAC is the legal company commander but he or she also works through the cadet company commander. The TAC's primary duty is to develop leadership in upperclass cadets and also to serve as a counselor and adviser to all the cadets in the company.

The Academy expects cadet officers to handle the guidance and direction for fourth- and third-class cadets before a problem is addressed by the company commander or the TAC.

Leadership is developed early. If a cadet has a problem, then he or she is expected to go the first level in the chain of command, the team leader, who is a Yearling. The team leaders work with the Plebes on issues ranging from military bearing and grades to the Plebe's home life, and how the fourth-class cadet is handling stress. Team leaders listen closely, gather information about the situation, and counsel fellow cadets on the Military Academy services and systems available to assist with their problems.

Early leadership and mentoring occurs as a one-to-one event. Every Yearling has one Plebe in his or her immediate charge. "It's my job to teach my Plebe how to do it right, and that also means how to stay out of trouble," says a Yearling. "If a Plebe doesn't learn soon enough that his salute should be sharper, his room must be squared away, and he better have the right answers to an upperclass's questions, then he's looking for trouble and a Heat Magnet will find him."

At the next level, all squad leaders and platoon sergeants are Cows. If a situation involves a difficult relationship between the cadet and another classmate, the team leader is expected to use appropriate leadership behavior to resolve the problem. But if the problem is more difficult than the team leader can solve, it is routed to the squad leader, the platoon sergeant next, and then the platoon leader. Cadets succeed when they lead others effectively and they operate as a team. That is why team leaders handle problems with cadets in their charge first, because that Yearling or Cow will be responsible someday for similar and perhaps more significant issues that affect the soldiers in his or her command.

Cadets candidly describe the things they like least at the Academy. They grow weary from the constant state of regimentation, but they know that order is intrinsic to an effective military environment. Another problem is the Corps' isolation. "We're so removed from the public. They don't have a broad understanding of Academy life," remarked a cadet. "The paradox is that we would like outsiders to know more about us, but that isn't possible. Meanwhile, they usually form opinions and make judgments when they hear something about West Point in the news or watch us in review on the Plain. We're a lot more than parades and news bites."

The seasons also affect the mood of the cadets. Typically, bleak skies, barren tree branches, New York's cold winters, and the melancholy gray color of the barracks and other Academy buildings can cast a collective pall on the institution's grounds. Cadets call the months from January until March the "gloom period."

But just as easily the cadets find aspects of West Point that they admire. They like the broad educational curriculum; they appreciate the variety of professional development experiences in the Army's service branches they participate in during summer training. "I like the fact that the work ethic is strong here," said one Firstie. "Cadets are seldom from wealthy families. Most cadets come from the middle- and lower-middle socioeconomic classes. They come from homes where there's a solid work ethic. When they get here, they really see the value of the work ethic to us as individuals and when we work together."

Another Firstie remarked: "West Point does more than tell you what is morally and ethically right about the way you conduct yourself as a person and as a future officer. The instructors reinforce those principles in class and in the field."

A Yearling said that she liked the diverse backgrounds of her classmates and that the Academy mandates that cadets "understand each other." She continued: "I like our company cohesion meetings. We eat meals together, face common problems together, talk about our futures together. It strengthens the common mission that all of us share."

The U.S. Military Academy's strategic guidance plan, *West Point: 2002 and Beyond*, couldn't agree more. It governs the education and training of the entire Corps of Cadets. The document explains how the West Point graduates who will become the Army's second lieutenants and career officers in the twenty-first century will be expected to demonstrate assured leadership during unpredictable situations and uncertain times. They will have to apply creative skills to formulate sensible solutions to situations and to execute their plans with a firmness of purpose. They will also have to be highly effective communicators who understand human nature and respect the multicultural diversity of the soldiers whom they will command.

Cadets balance their academic, physical, and military training with extracurricular activities. Under the control of the Directorate of Cadet Activities, West Pointers can choose from among ninety clubs and teams that offer many social, cultural, athletic, religious, intellectual, and USCC support activities. Twenty-nine of those clubs are related to academics. Cadets can participate on the debate team, in foreign language clubs, behavioral science and leadership seminars, the Big Brother/Big Sister program, or study U.S. and international foreign policy through the domestic affairs and West Point forums and the Student Conference on U.S. Affairs.

The Cadet Fine Arts Forum sponsors professional art, music, dance, and drama programs for cadets and outside audiences. The Cadet Glee Club performs across the country. The Cadet Band plays at concerts, rallies, and athletic competitions. WKDT is the cadet-run full-service radio station for music, news, sports, and corps information. Cadets who are skilled photographers and journalists can work on five major cadet publications: The Howitzer, West Point's yearbook; The Pointer, the humorous satiric magazine; Bugle Notes, the basic fourth-class guide; The Mortar, a journal of cadet field training; and The Circle in the Spiral, a literary magazine. The Drill Team and cadet "Rabble Rousers"—cheerleaders and mule riders—lead Academy spirit at athletic events.

Cadets can also join mountaineering, white-water canoe, ski, off-road bike, and model railroad clubs. Others sign up for sailing, sport parachuting, team handball, bowling, crew, skeet and trap shooting, riding, and fencing. Club teams compete against other collegiate and civilian teams, as well as in regional and national championships.

The Academy's strategic guidance statement stresses that spiritual development and opportunities for religious growth are a prominent aspect of cadet life. The proximity of the different cadet chapels to daily cadet traffic symbolizes the significance of spiritual development in the West Point experience. Cadets are strongly encouraged to attend worship services, and cadet chapel choirs participate in weekly services. Cadets volunteer to teach Sunday School and religious education classes for the children and youth on the Post. Some of the specific activity groups are the Officers Christian Fellowship, Jewish Chapel Choir, Cadet Catholic Folk Group, Gospel Choir, Baptist Student Union, and Fellowship of Christian Athletes.

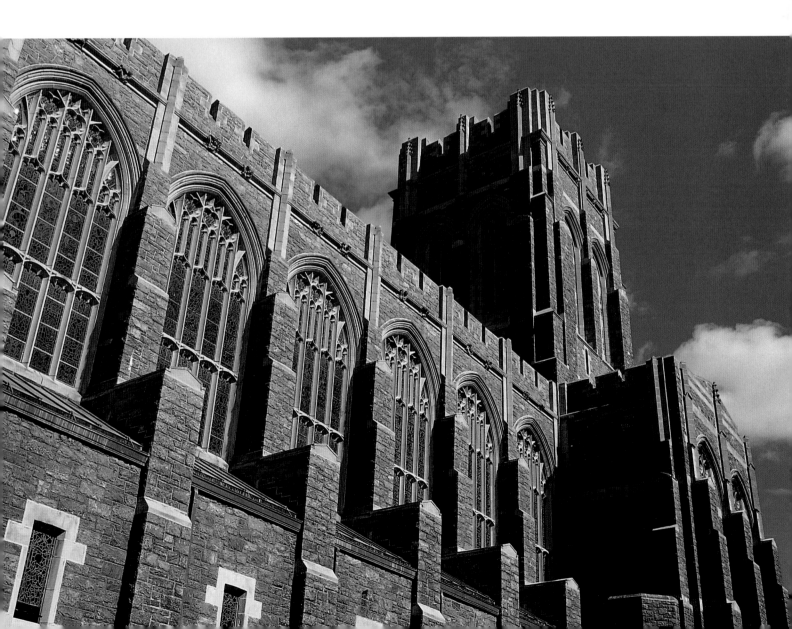

*   *   *

Several thousand spectators come to West Point each year to watch the Corps of Cadets pass in parade review on the Plain. In the fall, cadet reviews take place every Saturday morning before home football games. In the spring—starting in April and ending with graduation week in June—the cadets will pass in review as many as twelve times. Most reviews involve the entire brigade; at other times, though, the reviews are limited to two of the four regiments.

When the review begins, the regiments march simultaneously from their barracks areas through the four sally ports that lead out onto the Plain and in front of Washington Hall and the monument that honors Gen. George Washington. Unveiled in 1916, the statue of Washington seated proudly on horseback is a striking backdrop for every review. After the color guard comes out, the first captain's staff calls all four regiments through close-order drills. When they are finished, each of the thirty-six companies passes in review before the superintendent, the commandant, and other visiting dignitaries. The cadet company officers (all first-class cadets) wear red sashes and carry sabers. The rest of the company's cadets are always "under arms," that is, with their rifles.

*"A humorous event
I'll always remember
about academy life?
Nothing funny about that place."*

Gen. Arthur E. Brown, Jr., USA
(Ret.), USMA '53

*"The Beast Barracks order was to turn out in Dress Gray
with white gloves under arms.
One helpless Plebe proceeded to formation with his white gloves
precariously positioned in his armpits."*

Col. Charles A. Crowe, USA (Ret.), USMA '51

Dress uniform for review is Full Dress Gray. The exception is during regimental reviews in the spring when the cadets don Full Dress Gray Over White, under arms. The all-wool Full Dress Gray uniform coat is comfortable in winter, but it can be intolerable in hot and humid weather. Sometimes the heat is so overwhelming that a cadet will drop while standing in formation on the Plain.

Rank has its privileges. Periods of leave and free time are more available for upper-class cadets than for Plebes. All cadets are granted leave for Thanksgiving (about four days) and Christmas (about three weeks), but only the third, second, and first classes are allowed Spring Leave. While they are away, the Plebes remain at West Point for Plebe Parent Week, in March, which immediately follows Recognition Week. At that time, they assume the chain-of-command positions and run the Corps.

Plebes are allowed one weekend pass per semester; many of them combine that single pass with one of several three-day weekends, such as Labor Day. All cadets can earn Performance Passes for outstanding performance in the academic, military, or physical disciplines. While upperclass cadets may leave the Post in civilian clothes, Plebes must always depart in the appropriate seasonal uniform. Firsties earn four passes, while Cows earn three and Yearlings two per semester.

When Army intercollegiate teams compete against another service Academy, the cadets plan and participate in different activities the week of the contest to raise team spirit and enthusiasm for the event. For football contests, the cadets wear their BDUs for the entire week preceding the Saturday game. Spirits are raised at bonfires and pep rallies, team send-offs, and parades. For the Army-Navy football game, the cadets engage in a "goat-engineer" football contest as well as the spirit run, when cadets run the game ball from West Point to the playing field (often in Philadelphia).

The Army-Navy football game, played the first Saturday of December, is one of *the* most famous college football classics in the United States. The contest, first played in 1890, is the season finale for both academies. The entire Corps of Cadets and the Brigade of Midshipmen from the U.S. Naval Academy attend the game. Every year, groups from both sides engage in some mischievous pranks: taunting the opposite side, stealing banners, and hanging stuffed-toy mascots—goats and mules—in effigy. The rivalry was so intense one year that cadets kidnapped Navy's mascot, Bill the Goat. In 1991 the midshipmen got even. During a midnight expedition to West Point, they kidnapped Army's mules and showcased them back in Annapolis forty-eight hours before the game. The commandants from both academies eventually signed an agreement stating that neither school would allow any attempts to kidnap the other's mascot.

West Point, together with the Naval, Air Force, and Coast Guard Academies, participates annually in a student exchange program. Hundreds of cadets and midshipmen apply each year, but only up to ten final candidates are selected. The designated students study and live at the sister school of their choice during the fall semester of their second-class year. At the Naval Academy in Annapolis, Maryland, for example, a cadet becomes a temporary, yet active, member of the Brigade of Midshipmen. During the school day, he or she is identified in an As For Class uniform, while the mids are in their "working blues"; for parades on Worden Field the cadet would be seen in his or her Full Dress Gray uniform.

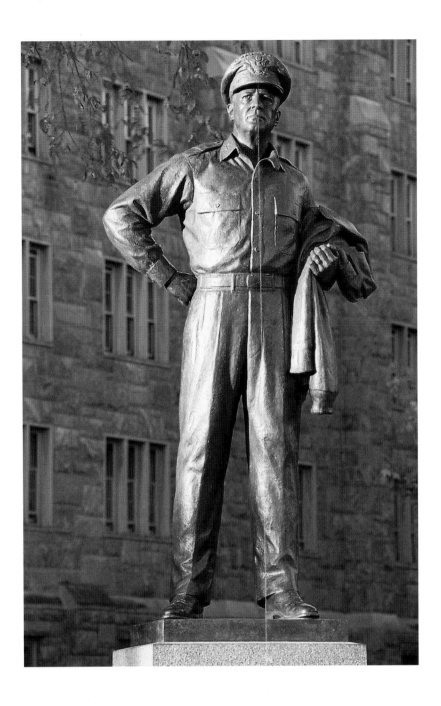

* * *

The honor code at West Point addresses three main goals for cadets' ethical and moral development. First, the essential duty of a leader to establish a healthy ethical climate within a unit; second, understanding how important integrity is to effective leadership; and third, maintaining an honorable lifestyle that demonstrates the spirit of the honor code. The honor code states, "A cadet will not lie, cheat or steal nor tolerate those who do." Cadets cannot deviate from these standards at any time, whether they are in or out of uniform.

Colonel Pappas writes that the formal inception of honor as part of cadet leadership may have started as early as the period when Sylvanus Thayer, as superintendent, believed that discipline in the Corps of Cadets was very important, and he began to incorporate changes involving violations, reporting of excuses, and punishment.

After World War I General Douglas MacArthur worked to formalize the code and system at the Academy which, in 1926, became the official sanctions for building integrity and character. Cadets really advanced their active role in reviewing all honor offenses after MacArthur left West Point. The cadet-led honor system continues today. The Douglas MacArthur Memorial, dedicated on September 12, 1969, is located near the MacArthur Barracks and across the street from the superintendent's quarters. A graduate of the USMA Class of 1903, MacArthur was appointed superintendent after World War I. The base of the statue is inscribed with passages from MacArthur's famous farewell speech to the Corps of Cadets in 1962, which prominently cites the Academy motto: Duty, Honor, Country.

Each cadet is personally responsible for his or her conduct and is expected to report any other cadet who has violated it. Cadets who break the code are separated or expelled permanently from the Academy. West Point and the Department of the Army assume shared responsibility for the conduct and application of the honor system. The Cadet Honor Committee is the initial and primary group that evaluates all reported honor code violations. Each of the thirty-six companies has two honor representatives who serve as advisors to the committee.

Bugle Notes lists the "Three Rules of Thumb" of the honor system, rules designed to help cadets decide if a given action that is likely to be committed falls within the bounds of the honorable behavior expected of all cadets. The rules, as stated in *Bugle Notes*, are:

> 1. Does this action attempt to deceive anyone or allow anyone to be deceived?
> 2. Does this action gain or allow the gain of a privilege or advantage to which I or someone else would not otherwise be entitled?
> 3. Would I be satisfied by the outcome if I were on the receiving end of this action?

> The purpose of the United States Military Academy is 'to provide the nation with leaders of character who serve the common defense.' The purpose of the Cadet Honor Code is to foster in each cadet a commitment to moral-ethical excellence essential to being a leader of character. The Honor Code is, therefore, the cornerstone of the Academy environment. . . .

West Point's honor system is unique among the service academies because it stresses that loyalty to honorable conduct and the values of the institution must be higher than loyalty to one's peers, if their conduct is clearly dishonorable. Although intolerance of observed violations was not officially added to the code until 1970, cadets have practiced it throughout most of the Academy's history.

A trademark of the Academy's honor system is the Cadet Honor Education Program. This four-year program begins during Cadet Basic Training, when new cadets attend seminars with such titles as "The Honor System at West Point," "Truthfulness, Fairness, Respect for Others' Property, Non-toleration and 'Identity,'" and "The Honor Investigative Hearing." Third-class cadets study "Field Honor," "Honor and the Professional Army Officer," and "The Role of the Small Unit Leader in Honor."
In each academic term cadets attend honor education courses that range from "Applications of Honorable Living in Cadet Life," "Introduction to the Ethical Dilemma," and "Courage and Candor," to "Establishing the Moral and Ethical Climate in the Field Army," and "Ethics in America—Under Orders, Under Fire."

Each class has different numbers of demerits they are allowed to accrue before being disciplined. Firsties have the fewest and Plebes have the most. A cadet can be sanctioned with an area tour—walking a post for a determined number of hours—if he or she exceeds their monthly total of allowed demerits, or if that cadet's tactical officer feels the discipline is justified. Area tours are imposed for minor offenses, like failing to make a bed, and more serious ones, such as leaving a post without authorization or missing a formation. Cadets serve area tours in Central Area, where they march back and forth, carrying their rifles at right or left shoulder arms. All cadets wait through a long inspection before they serve their tours.

The most difficult part for cadets about walking tours and room restrictions is that the punishment takes away a cadet's free time, a valuable entitlement. Their peers at civilian universities, say cadets, cannot understand nor can they appreciate how precious free time is in a cadet's daily life.

All area tours are conducted on the weekends; cadets can usually walk off up to five hours during a Saturday and a Sunday.

A momentous event for the graduating class of cadets occurs every January: branch selection. Assignments are based on several factors, including: cadet rank at the end of a first-class cadet's seventh semester; Department of the Army guidance on the number of slots available for each of the service's sixteen branches; and the individual cadet's branch preferences.

Cadets who are not physically qualified for combat branches are, of necessity, limited to those in noncombat areas. On Branch Notification Night, the first class receives its branch assignments. Instead of mandatory dinner that evening, the entire first class forms up in their regimental areas and marches down to the Eisenhower Hall theater. Seated in their companies, they listen to a speech by the Commandant of Cadets, then the first captain orders the four regimental commanders to pick up their boxes containing envelopes to pass to each company commander. When the envelopes are finally distributed, the first captain orders the cadets to open the envelopes and find in them the brass insignia representing their chosen or assigned branch. Firsties are usually confident that the majority of them will receive one of the three branches they selected earlier in September.

The branches are: IN—Infantry; AR—Armor; FA—Field Artillery; AD—Air Defense Artillery; EN—Engineers; AV—Aviation; SC—Signal Corps; MP—Military Police; MI—Military Intelligence; AG—Adjutant Generals Corps; FI—Finance Corps; MS—Medical Service Corps; CM—Chemical Corps; TC—Transportation; OD—Ordnance; and QM—Quartermaster.

In April 1812 Congress ordered that "Cadets heretofore appointed in the service of the United States, whether of artillery, cavalry, riflemen, or infantry, or that may in the future be appointed . . . be attached at the discretion of the President of the United States, as students to the Military Academy." Any cadet who received a regular academic degree and attended all classes was to "be considered as among the candidates for a commission in any corps, according to the duties he may be judged competent to perform."

The majority of male cadets in a recent graduating class selected infantry, armor, field artillery, aviation, and engineering. Among the females the preferred choices were military intelligence, aviation, military police, and quartermaster. Army regulations still do not allow women to serve in the infantry or armor divisions, but they are admitted into some areas of field artillery. Women also fly helicopters in combat in the Army.

Near Michie Stadium, the American soldier's statue symbolizes the institution's principle of service to country. It was presented by the Classes of 1935 and 1936 to West Point in 1980 and honors American soldiers who lost their lives in combat.

PRESENTED TO THE CORPS OF CADETS

THE LIVES AND DESTINIES OF VALIANT AMERICANS
ARE ENTRUSTED TO YOUR CARE AND LEADERSHIP.

CLASS OF 1935   CLASS OF 1936

FELIX DE WELDON SCULPTOR 1910

TO THE AMERICAN SOLDIER

The cadets adjourn to Eisenhower Hall's restaurant for refreshments after the assignments have been read. There, each branch is represented with brochures and other specific information, and many active-duty officers are present to welcome cadets who will join their branches in June. During the evening celebration, most cadets will affix their branch insignia to their uniform. Sometimes they attach it directly to their skin and call it the "blood branch."

Approximately one month after Branch Notification Night, the Post Selection Ceremony takes place. Cadets name the U.S. Army installation where they want to go for their branch training.

Ring Weekend at West Point is held in late August each year. The weekend's activities commemorate Firsties receiving a class ring, an honored occasion that originated with the Class of 1835. Each West Point class designs its crest, and the ring bears the class crest on one side and the Academy crest on the other. The cadets choose their stone and setting design.

Ring Weekend starts on Friday afternoon with the Ring Ceremony. The Firsties march out by company on to the Plain in their India White uniforms. After the first captain presents the class to the superintendent and the commandant, the class breaks ranks into two groups that march down behind Battle Monument at Trophy Point to the area overlooking a panoramic view of the Hudson River for a private ceremony. Dedicated in 1897, the monument honors the men and officers of the Regular Army who were killed in the Civil War. The names of these men are inscribed on the ornaments; the statue that represents "Fame" is at the highest point of the tall marble column.

When the ceremony ends, a mass of proud and smiling Firsties rises up over the crest of the hill at Trophy Point. As they walk across the Plain and approach Washington Hall, the newly ringed cadets become the center of attention for some spirited West Point fun. Teams of Plebes, five to ten together, run up and surround the Firstie, drop to one knee, and chant together the "Ring Poop": Oh my God, sir/ma'am! What a beautiful ring! What a crass mass of brass and glass! What a bold mold of rolled gold! See how it sparkles and shines! It must have cost you a fortune! May I touch it please, sir/ma'am?"

On Saturday evening, cadets and their dates assemble in Cadet Mess at 7:00 P.M. for the Ring Banquet. Afterward, the Firsties walk over to Eisenhower Hall for their hop. The commandant and his wife meet each couple, photographers capture beaming couples on film in front of a large model of the ring, and everyone celebrates.

III

SUMMER
TRAINING

"During the Vietnam conflict, I had the honor of commanding an infantry battalion and an infantry brigade. I attribute the success achieved to the unique character of the overall educational experience at the U.S. Military Academy. . . . This experience has convinced me that the broad aspects of service academy training are designed to prepare young men and women to command in time of war."

Gen. Alexander M. Haig, Jr., USA (Ret.), USMA '47

Starting with Cadet Basic Training, each cadet's academic semesters and the summer months between them involve him or her in a comprehensive program of military classroom and field training. Baseline requirements in the military program are centered on three core components: military training, military science, and professional development. Military training encompasses the four summer field training programs that cadets must successfully complete. Under the classification of military science, cadets of each class attend courses during the spring semester and also the intersession between the Christmas holiday and the following academic period. The courses cover military heritage and professionalism, tactics, military knowledge and skills, ethics, and communications skills. In professional development, cadets attend discussions and briefings on human relations, honor/moral development, duty concept, alcohol/drug abuse, and leader training.

After the end of the Civil War, up to the early 1940s, cadets of all four classes conducted summer military training at a camp near Fort Clinton, and near the Plain. The branches in the profession of arms during this period were field engineering, artillery, cavalry, and infantry. Cadets learned some ordnance, but these lessons were presented primarily during the academic periods.

In general, courses in military science and leadership cover small unit tactics and leadership. The physical education program prepares cadets for the rigors of service life and combat readiness. Field training at Army units during the summer period is planned so cadets will apply and practice leadership at the unit level, a consideration for others, personal accountability for decisions and consequences, confidence, and interpersonal skills.

* * *

During Beast Barracks, new cadets have their first direct experiences with soldier training and skills performance in the field of combat. Training is based on the Army's Military Qualification Standard (MQS) system. Outfitted in camouflage combat gear, they
take Basic Rifle Marksmanship I (BRM) and receive briefings on the characteristics
and safety features of their weapon, the M-16A2 semi-automatic rifle. The Cadet
Cadre teach them how to load and unload the rifle, how to make sight adjustments,
and how to fire from combat positions. During BRM II, they load their M-16 rifles
with live ammunition and fire from foxholes at targets twenty-five meters away. Later,
they advance to the Remotely Engaged Targeting System Range, where they fire forty
rounds of ammunition and engage forty target exposures at ranges of fifty to three
hundred meters: twenty from the prone position (supported by sandbags) and twenty
from the unsupported position, both in and out of the foxhole.

The new cadets' training continues as they learn to use hand grenades, practicing first with fake ones and then live grenades. At Individual Tactical Training, or ITT, upperclass members of the Cadet Cadre teach new cadets to camouflage themselves and their equipment, to develop a survival plan, to move under direct fire, move over, through, or around obstacles, react to indirect fire, and to prepare squad/platoon combat orders. They also participate in all-night bivouacs on the "reservation" (another term that refers to the entire West Point Post) and at Lake Frederick, and teamwork is stressed during athletic competitions and at the Leadership Reaction Course and Confidence Obstacle Course.

Third-class cadets have seven weeks of military field training, called Cadet Field Training, or CFT, at Camp Buckner. Their trainers and senior leaders at Buckner are first- and second-class cadets who are assisted by Army troop units representing different specialty branches. The experience is a physically and mentally strenuous period for the Yearlings as they learn and practice firsthand simulations of real-life military situations. At Buckner, they receive their first exposure to several Army field branches. Training covers infantry operations, weapons, artillery firing, Army aviation, field communications, military engineering, and survival practices. For example, cadets at engineer train-

ing work with fixed and floating bridges, they learn mine and countermine warfare, and they practice demolition and field engineering tasks such as building field fortifications and obstacles against an enemy ground attack.

The bayonet assault course is a demanding introduction to infantry, leadership, and quick thinking under fire. During weapons training, cadets fire the direct and indirect fire weapons associated with the Light Infantry companies. They qualify on the M-16 semi-automatic rifle after completing the marksmanship training, and they learn to fire an M-60 machine gun, the LAW (light anti-tank weapon), a grenade launcher, and mortars. The communications course introduces third-class cadets to the skills, procedures, and equipment that apply to modern battlefield communications. Finally, cadets must demonstrate proficiency in map and terrain reading and using a compass at night as well as in the daytime.

While they are training at Camp Buckner, third-class cadets participate in Soldier Fitness Day. The series of innovative platoon-level and mission-related tasks are designed to physically challenge the cadets and to emphasize teamwork, communications, and successfully completing a mission under time limits and physical fatigue. To simulate field artillery, one platoon team must disassemble all four tubes of an 81-mm mortar, carry the heavy pieces across a field, sprint with them to the top of a hill, reassemble them without sighting, then break the mortars down again, carry them back down the hill, and finally reassemble them on the field under tight time constraints. Meanwhile, the other platoon team uses ropes to pull a two-and-a-half ton truck across a field and up a hill to their mission position.

"I knew that my decision to attend West Point was right when I and one-third of my class were sent directly to the Korean conflict without any branch schooling. While I commanded a recoilless rifle platoon—and I had never fired that particular weapon—I relied on my military and leadership training at West Point to form an effective platoon and to aid them in surviving hard combat during those days on the Pusan Perimeter in 1950."

Col. William B. DeGraf, USA (Ret.),
USMA '50

At the Litter Obstacle Course, platoon members simulate transporting comrades injured in battle. Teams of two must carry another platoon member on a litter as they negotiate a difficult obstacle course in the woods in a certain length of time. At the Fighting Position Construction, a platoon must break down one field infantry bunker position of five hundred sandbags, transport the bags one at a time across a field to a designated defensive position, and quickly rebuild the bunker.

Another challenging event is the battleground engineering mission. After receiving instructions from Army enlisted trainers, platoon teams race against the clock, carrying very heavy pieces of equipment to a ravine and constructing a bridge over it. Also, all West Point cadets must successfully complete the Slide for Life. They walk across a beam suspended thirty feet over the lake, then they jump to catch a rope, and, finally, drop into the water. These water-confidence courses represent battlefield conditions.

Yearlings spend one week at Fort Knox, Kentucky, for the Mounted Maneuver Training phase of CFT. There cadets learn about armor, mechanized infantry, air defense operations, combat engineering, and self-propelled field artillery. For example, during the field artillery exercises cadets perform the duties of firing battery personnel; they learn how to conduct reconnaissance, followed by selecting and occupying a battery position; and they learn how to employ field artillery that supports infantry and armor units. Army officers at Fort Knox teach cadets the relationship between small unit ground combat operations and their military instruction lessons at West Point. Third-class military science instruction on combined arms operations concentrates on company-team and task force operations.

Second-class cadets can select from two training options. While each option broadens the cadet's military training, the one which the cadet chooses will determine his or her first-class summer professional training experience.

The first option is five weeks at Drill Cadet Leader Training. Cadets are stationed at one of the Army's six training centers in the United States, where they direct enlisted personnel in Army units. Next, they participate in a two- to three-week Individual Advanced Development assignment. Their choices are: Northern Warfare Operations, in Alaska; Mountain Warfare, in Vermont; Airborne, at Fort Benning, Georgia; Air Deployment Planning and Surface Deployment Planning, at Fort Eustis, Virginia; Air Assault, at Camp Smith, New York; Sapper Training at Fort Leonard Wood, Missouri; and the legendary and difficult Survival, Evasion, Resistance, and Escape training at the U.S. Air Force Academy in Colorado Springs, Colorado.

In the second training option, cadets serve for five weeks as squad leaders for Cadet Basic Training and also for Cadet Field Training. When that assignment is finished, they select an Individual Advanced Development specialty for two to three weeks. Second-class cadets also receive military science training that covers platoon readiness, platoon leader duties for maintaining unit readiness, and briefing techniques.

Only a limited number of second-class cadets go to Army bases. Most participate in military development at West Point and assigned locations elsewhere. Cows can spend their second-class summer serving internships at the Pentagon, participating in triathlon training in Lake Placid, New York, assigned to the Department of Physical Education at West Point, or studying environmental sciences.

First-class cadets who selected Drill Cadet Leader Training the previous summer serve five weeks in a leadership role for either CBT or CFT. Meanwhile, the Firsties who spent their second-class summer training new cadets or leading third-class summer training attend a five-week Cadet Troop Leader Training at a U.S. Army post in either Alaska, Hawaii, and the continental United States or overseas in Germany, Panama, or Korea. All first-class cadets also attend two to three weeks of Individual Advanced Development training in an Army specialty.

When the Firsties return to West Point to begin their last academic year, many are selected to assume leadership roles from the brigade and regimental levels to the platoon level. Others manage the activities of the cadets. First-class military education continues with courses on military justice, ethics, Army organization, platoon management and leadership, terrorism protection measures, and the role of the noncommissioned officer.

IV

COMMISSIONING WEEK

"On a visit to West Point after graduation, I finally had time to look around, reflect on what I saw, and take everything in. I thought about all the great soldiers who had preceded me—Generals Bradley, Grant, Lee, MacArthur, Patton, Pershing, and Sherman. It was overpowering, and I was immensely proud to be a part of The Long Gray Line."

Hope Donnelly, USMA '86

A week of special events in late May/early June leads up to the day when first-class members of the Corps of Cadets graduate and receive commissions as second lieutenants in the United States Army.

Early in graduation week, the Alumni Ceremony and Review takes place. A procession of the oldest living West Point graduates marches along Diagonal Walk in the morning to a wreath-laying ceremony at Thayer Monument, near the superintendent's quarters. It is a timeless moment as the first captain, representing the current generation of West Pointers, salutes and shakes hands with the oldest living graduate—someone who may be two generations older. Later that morning, the full brigade passes in review before the alumni and the public.

At the annual Awards Convocation, those graduating cadets who have achieved outstanding marks in academics and military and physical development are honored in a public ceremony. The five-point gold star is awarded to cadets of distinguished academic excellence. A gold wreath goes to recipients of the Superintendent's Award, cadets who were named to the Dean's List and also excelled in military and physical performance events.

The day before graduation, the cadets of the fourth, third, and second classes pass in review before the first-class cadets at the Graduation Parade. When the Firsties march through the sally ports of Washington Hall and out onto the Plain before the other classes appear, it is the last time these senior cadets stand in their Full Dress Gray uniforms on West Point's parade field.

The graduation banquet and the graduation hop are conducted the evening before graduation. Accompanied by their dates, graduating cadets dressed in India White uniforms celebrate their final official dinner and social event as West Point cadets.

Until the early 1900s, graduation was conducted in front of the old chapel. The Chairman of the Board of Visitors gave a short speech and handed out diplomas. When West Point graduate, General of the Army, and President of the United States Ulysses S. Grant came to address the graduates, Academy officials moved the event to the Plain. Theodore Roosevelt was the first American president to oversee the cadets' graduation and commissioning, and the ceremony moved at that time to Cullum Hall. Eventually, by the 1930s, graduating classes grew so large that the ceremony had to be moved to the Battle Monument at Trophy Point, and finally to Michie Stadium.

Graduation-address speakers rotate between the President and Vice President of the United States, the Secretary of the Army, and distinguished military leaders and government figures. When the address is finished, the guest speaker, the Superintendent of the U.S. Military Academy, the Dean of the Academic Board, and the Commandant of Cadets present diplomas to the members of the graduating class. It is an emotional moment as cadets walk down the ramp with their diploma in hand and hug fellow company members. Others hold their diplomas high in the air and look in the direction of family and friends seated in the stadium.

*"Almost thirty years after graduation, while attending a leadership institute,
I was given one hour to write a paper concerning the principles and ethics by which
I live my life. I wrote only three words: Duty, Honor, Country."*

Gen. H. Norman Schwarzkopf, USA(Ret.), USMA '56

After the Corps of Cadets sing their alma mater, graduates stand with white-gloved
right hands raised and repeat the Oath of Office administered by the superintendent.

I [name], having been appointed an officer in the United States Army in
the grade of Second Lieutenant, do solemnly swear that I will support
and defend the Constitution of the United States against all enemies,
foreign and domestic; that I will bear true faith and allegiance to the
same; that I take this obligation freely without any mental reservation or
purpose of evasion; and that I will well and faithfully discharge the
duties of the office upon which I am about to enter, so help me God.

When the Academy chaplain has finished giving the benediction, the graduates carry out one of the most anticipated moments of the occasion. In one burst of simultaneous energy—accompanied by shouts and cheers—the graduates fill the sky with West Point white-uniform hats as they toss them high into the air, never to wear them again. Their long, arduous journey at West Point is over. Now they are graduates of the United States Military Academy and will join the ranks of Generals MacArthur, Lee, Eisenhower, Patton, Sheridan, Bradley, and thousands of other graduates who served as Army officers.

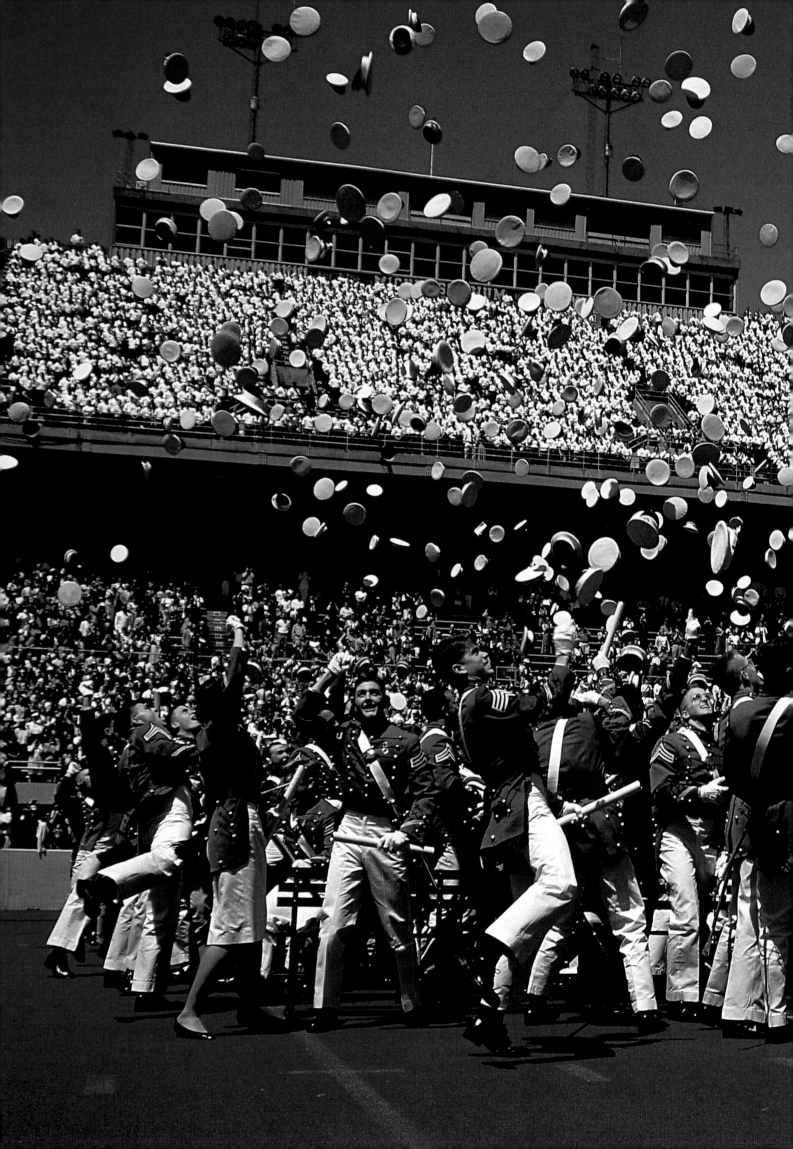

The moment the hats start falling to the ground, the stadium traditionally fills with children who run out to pick them up as souvenirs. Meanwhile, the Cows who were assigned as ushers and escorts for the graduation ceremony also fulfill a traditional rite of passage. The second-class cadets are now officially the Academy's Firsties. They share a proud moment too as classmates team up and flip over one another's first-class epaulets.

After the stadium empties, graduates—now dressed in their Army officer uniforms—assemble with family members and friends at various locations on the Academy grounds. A designated person will pin the gold second lieutenant bars on the new officer's uniform coat.

Moments after graduation, many cadets are lined up near the Cadet Chapel, waiting to be married. Because a chapel wedding is so revered, reservations have to be made at least one year in advance. The wedding party and the newlyweds always leave the chapel and pass through the traditional arch of swords raised by the groom's sword bearers.

Graduating cadets typically have several thoughts as they leave the U.S. Military Academy. Beast Barracks and Plebe Year happened an eternity ago, but somehow it seems like yesterday. Some aspects of West Point were unpleasant, a few were dreadful, but the nice memories are numerous. Four difficult years have just ended. Now, the graduating class is expected to serve as ably as the lineage of Army officers from prior classes did. They too must carry on the tradition of The Long Gray Line from West Point.

APPENDIX

1900   (U.S. MILITARY ACADEMY ARCHIVES)

UNIFORMS

In 1814 the official cadet uniform was a dark blue coat over gray trousers in the summer, dark blue coats with dark blue trousers in winter. At the time, durable blue wool was hard to acquire due to restrictions from the War of 1812. Two years later the third Superintendent of the U.S. Military Academy, Col. Joseph G. Swift, recommended that the gray uniform should become the permanent cadet uniform. "The price of the uniform $18 to $20 better suits the finance of the Cadets than one of Blue wool."

Uniforms today are an area of Academy life that is tightly regulated. Cadets must consult "The United States Corps of Cadets Regulations" to find out when it is appropriate to wear the Gray Jacket, an overgarment and uniform accessory. For example, it can be worn with the White Over Gray uniform while cadets are on the Post, when the weather is unseasonably cold. "The gray jacket will be zipped completely closed, except with the long-sleeve class shirt . . . it will be zipped to within a three finger width distance from the top, and is not authorized as an outer garment when eating a meal in the mess hall, except when authorized by the company commander."

In fact, cadets cannot personally decide on the outer garment to wear when they leave their barracks room in the morning. Uniform flags that identify the appropriate outer garment to wear are posted at several locations in Central Area.

> Red = overcoat/field jacket (when combined with the camouflage flag)
> Black = raincoat
> Green = overshoes
> Camouflage = BDU
> Red square on green background = gray jacket
> Black diagonal on white background = parka

Uniform regulations address just about every conceivable situation relating to the dress code, and they vary from significant to minor. For example, when headgear can and cannot be removed; what to wear while sunbathing on the Post or watching athletic competitions; when to wear gloves or carry book bags.

Besides the class rank identifications—namely, the number of stars on shirt collars, insignia on shoulder boards, and chevrons on dress coat sleeves—cadets proudly wear their U.S. Military Academy awards on their uniforms. A West Pointer designated a "Distinguished Cadet" for academic excellence wears a five-point star; a Superintendent's Award for overall excellence earns the cadet a decorative wreath. Athletes also wear their letters, monograms, and other decorations, including a large "Major A" chenille letter worn on gray jackets and black cardigan sweaters. Army athletes who have competed against the Naval and Air Force Academies and won earn some of West Point's most coveted awards.

Cadets wear eleven primary uniforms:

Full Dress Gray is the winter uniform worn to formal occasions such as banquets, dances, parades, and ceremonies. The Full Dress Hat, with a plume that designates cadet rank, or the gray service hat is always worn with this uniform. Women cannot wear gray skirts with this uniform when they are in formations or when the commandant has prescribed trousers. First-class cadets wear the red sash with the Full Dress Gray.

Full Dress Gray Over White is a formal uniform worn in the spring or fall, also for parades, ceremonies, and various social functions. This is usually prescribed for Graduation Week events. The Full Dress Hat with plume or the white service hat is always worn with this uniform.

Full Dress Gray (men's)

Full Dress Gray (women's)

Full Dress Gray Over White

India White

Dress Gray

Dress Gray Over White

India White is the formal summer season uniform that cadets wear to social functions, parades, and ceremonies instead of Full Dress Gray. A belt or a red sash, depending on the cadet's rank, is always worn with this uniform. White gloves and white hat are required with India White. As when cadets don the Full Dress Gray, the Commandant of Cadets may authorize them to remove their headgear when they attend certain functions.

Dress Gray is the standard cadet winter uniform. The official change-over to winter wear usually occurs on the first Monday in October and lasts until the first Monday in May. Cadets wear Dress Gray when they escort civilians and when they leave the Post, to evening lectures, and at weekend optional meals. The gray service hat is the required headgear.

White Over Gray   As For Class   Dress Mess

Dress Gray Over White is an optional uniform that may be worn in the spring or fall in lieu of White Over Gray when the weather is unseasonably cold. The gray service hat is always worn with this uniform.

White Over Gray is the standard summer uniform. Cadets wear this uniform while escorting visitors, departing the Post, and to evening lectures and mandatory dinners. The white service hat is always worn with White Over Gray.

As For Class is the standard class uniform for academic classes and it may be worn to optional dinner on weeknights. It is not permitted, however, when cadets attend an evening lecture or at any weekend optional meal or outside the academic/class area on weekends. The black shirts are short sleeved in the spring and summer seasons, long sleeved in the fall and winter seasons. Female cadets dressed in As For Class may wear skirts to class, meals, while performing Cadet in Charge of Quarters (CCQ) duties, and during off-duty periods, but they cannot wear skirts to drill, area tours, or guard duty. While they are not permitted to wear skirts for parades and ceremonies, they may wear them in meal and accountability formations. Skirts may be worn to the Graduation Ceremony.

With As For Class uniforms, cadet rank is identified by the West Point crest pin located on the left shirt collar. A Firstie's pin is the crest on a black field, a Cow's is on a silver field, a Yearling's is on a gold field; a Plebe does not wear an insignia pin. The same class insignias are worn on shoulder boards or epaulets of all India White, Dress Mess, and White Over Gray uniforms for the upper three classes.

Dress Mess is authorized for female cadets to wear to formal occasions such as banquets, hops, dining-ins, and other social situations. But Dress Mess is not allowed for reviews, ceremonies, or chapel services. Women do not need to wear headgear with this uniform, and they can wear pumps and carry a handbag.

| Battle Dress Uniform | Athletic Attire | Blazer Uniform |

Battle Dress Uniform, also known as BDU, is for field wear during summer training and for work details like moving into or out of a barracks room. It is the prescribed uniform for the period after the Christmas season holiday leave and before the second academic semester begins. The commandant usually designates BDU as the uniform for activities—such as pep rallies—that are connected to special athletic activities like the Army-Navy and Army–Air Force football games.

Athletic Attire comes in several forms. The primary athletic uniform is Gym Alpha. Regulations describe when this uniform is authorized or prohibited, depending on the time and the day, whether the cadet is inside or outside the barracks, and the kind of athletic or personal workout activity the cadet is participating in. Club or corps squad cadets may wear the DCA (Director of Cadet Athletics) or DIA (Director of Intercollegiate Athletics) team uniforms as they travel to and return from official practices and competitions. Besides Gym Alpha, other athletic wear includes the yellow running suit or the gray sweat shirt and pants issued to cadets.

Blazer Uniform is available for first-, second-, and third- class cadets to wear. The regulations specify that women may wear either a necktie or a scarf; men must wear a necktie—but not a bow tie—and the authorized class crest must be worn on the blazer uniform pocket.

ACKNOWLEDGMENTS

I am grateful to many individuals associated with West Point who extended to me their generous cooperation, interest, and support as I produced this book on the Corps of Cadets.

The members of the Military Academy Public Affairs staff, directed by Lt. Col. Donald J. McGrath, Jr., USA, became good friends and helpful advisers to me during my trips to West Point and Army units. I want to thank Don McGrath, Andrea Hamburger, Maj. Jay Ebbeson, and Theresa Ali for their valuable assistance and suggestions.

I owe Michael D'Aquino, who is the director of media relations at West Point's Public Affairs Office, my special gratitude. Mike recognized my determination to communicate West Point's story in words and dramatic photographs. He worked tirelessly to schedule my photo shoots and to coordinate important meetings and approvals for me with Army officers, from the company level in the USCC to the commandant's office. He was always at West Point to greet me on dark winter mornings when it seemed like the only people awake and dressed besides the two of us were four thousand cadets on their way to morning formation.

I received wonderful support from the Association of Graduates of The United States Military Academy, and I extend my sincere appreciation to this fine organization. Col. Seth F. Hudgins, Jr., USA (Ret.), president of the Association of Graduates, and Gregory H. Louks of the AOG staff provided valuable assistance and encouragement. Their friendship to me, as well as their belief that this book would contribute to West Point's esteemed place in our nation's history and future, was generous.

Finally, I want to thank several others who also were fine friends and helped me in many ways to succeed at my task. They are: Col. George S. Pappas, USA (Ret.), Lt. Col. William and Mrs. Jeanne Lambert, Paul W. Davison and Mark Walters (Class of 1995), Kate Ward and Scott Naumann (Class of 1996), and Steve Berlin (Class of 1997).

TECHNICAL DATA

Cameras: Nikon F3HP
Nikon N90 and N90s

Lenses: Nikkor 24mm F/2.8D AF
Nikkor 35mm F/2 AF
Nikkor 105mm F/2.5 AIS
Nikkor 180mm F/2.8 ED IF AF
Nikkor 80-200mm F/2.8D AF ED IF
Nikkor 300mm F/2.8 ED IF

Flash: Nikon SB-25 Speedlight

Films: Kodachrome PKL 200
Ektachrome Lumiere LPP and
  LPZ 100
Fujichrome Velvia 50
Fujichrome Sensia 100
Fujichrome Provia 100
Kodak Ektapress PJB 400
Fujicolor Super G 400
Fujicolor Super G 800

ABOUT THE AUTHOR

Robert Stewart has been a freelance journalist and an author of photo-documentary books for fifteen years. In 1993 he published *The Brigade in Review: A Year at the U.S. Naval Academy* (Naval Institute Press), illustrating in photographs and text the four-year preparation that midshipmen at the U.S. Naval Academy begin as plebes and finish as commissioned Navy and Marine Corps officers. In 1988 he published *Rowing: The Experience,* an all-color photo essay on the sport of competitive rowing in the United States. As a journalist, Mr. Stewart's assignments included hard news, investigative reporting, profiles, and special-section articles for publications including the *New York Times.* He lives in New Jersey with his family.

The **Naval Institute Press** is the book-publishing arm of the U.S. Naval Institute, a private, nonprofit society for sea service professionals and others who share an interest in naval and maritime affairs. Established in 1873 at the U.S. Naval Academy in Annapolis, Maryland, where its offices remain today, the Naval Institute has more than 85,000 members worldwide.

Members of the Naval Institute receive the influential monthly magazine *Proceedings* and discounts on fine nautical prints and on ship and aircraft photos. They also have access to the transcripts of the Institute's Oral History Program and get discounted admission to any of the Institute-sponsored seminars offered around the country. Discounts are also available to the colorful bimonthly magazine *Naval History*.

The Naval Institute's book-publishing program, begun in 1898 with basic guides to naval practices, has broadened its scope in recent years to include books of more general interest. Now the Naval Institute Press publishes about 100 titles each year, ranging from how-to books on boating and navigation to battle histories, biographies, ship and aircraft guides, and novels. Institute members receive discounts of 20 to 50 percent on the Press's nearly 600 books in print.

Full-time students are eligible for special half-price membership rates. Life memberships are also available.

For a free catalog describing Naval Institute Press books currently available, and for further information about joining the U.S. Naval Institute, please write to:

Membership Department
U.S. Naval Institute
118 Maryland Avenue
Annapolis, Maryland 21402-5035

Telephone: (800) 233-8764
Fax: (410) 269-7940